# Glow-in-the-Dark NIGHT FIGHTERS

THUNDERBOLT XG1

FIREFLY 41-X

Edited by Ben Grossblatt
Airplanes designed by Damon Brown
Book designed by Andrew Hess
Production management by Katie Stephens

becker&mayer!

Night Fighters is published by becker&mayer!
Copyright © 2004 becker&mayer!
11010 Northup Way, Bellevue, WA
www.beckermayer.com
If you have questions or comments about this product, send e-mail to infobm@beckermayer.com

Printed in China. ISBN 1-932855-09-2

03108

10 9 8 7 6 5 4 3 2 1

# Flying and Folding Tips

- When folding your planes, make sure the dashed lines are inside the fold. The dotted lines show you where the outside of the fold should be.
- Run your fingernail over the creases to make your folds extra smooth.
- Don't launch your plane directly at anyone, especially at anyone's face!
- If your plane dives (the nose goes down and the plane crashes), try making small, upward folds on the back edges of your plane's wings. A little fold goes a long way!
- If your plane stalls (the nose goes up, then the plane drops down and crashes), try making small downward folds on the back edges of the wings.
- Take any pointy-nosed airplane and fold the nose back about one inch. This makes the nose stronger so it can better survive crashes.
- Often a slower launch will work better than a really fast one.
- For planes that have wingtips (the Aurora and the Electric Bat), adjusting and refolding the tips can improve your flights. Making changes on the base of the Firefly will also affect its flight.
- Sometimes, a plane just turns out wrong, and no amount of tweaking, pinching, or re-folding will help. Recycle it, and try again!

# Thunderbolt

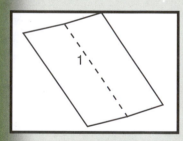

1. Fold paper in half length-wise along line 1, then unfold it.

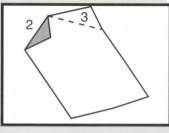

2. Fold corners in along lines 2 and 3.

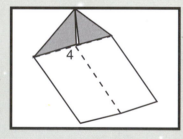

3. Fold tip up along line 4.

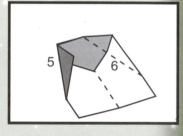

4. Fold corners in along lines 5 and 6.

5. Fold the small, center point down along line 7.

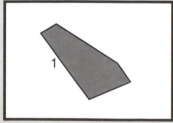

6. Fold plane in half again along line 1.

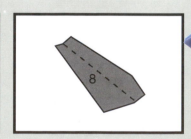

7. Fold wings down along lines 8 and 9.

**Finished Airplane**

# Aurora

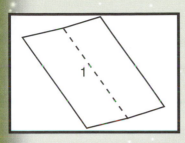

1. Fold paper in half length-wise along line 1, then unfold it.

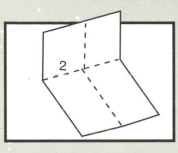

2. Fold one end up along line 2.

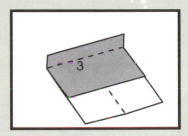

3. Now, fold up the same end along line 3.

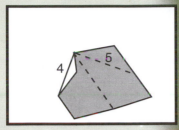

4. Turn the plane over. Fold the corners back along lines 4 and 5 so the edges meet in the middle.

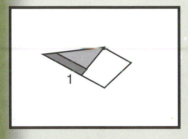

5. Flip the plane over again, and fold it in half again along line 1.

6. Fold the wings down along lines 6 and 7.

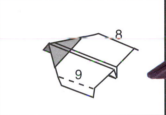

7. Fold the wing tips up along lines 8 and 9.

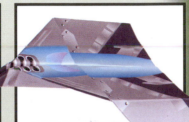

**Finished Airplane**

# Shooting Star

1. Fold paper in half along line 1, then unfold it.

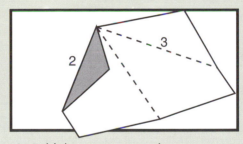

2. Fold the corners into the center, along lines 2 and 3.

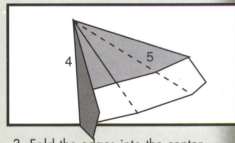

3. Fold the edges into the center again, along lines 4 and 5.

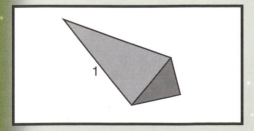

4. Turn the plane over and fold in half again, along line 1.

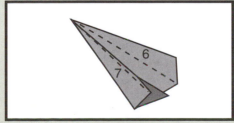

5. Fold down the wings, along lines 6 and 7.

**Finished Airplane**

# Electric Bat

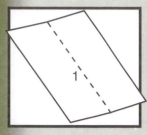

1. Fold paper in half length-wise along line 1, then unfold it.

2. Fold the corners in along lines 2 and 3.

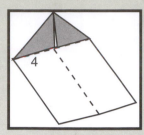

3. Fold tip up along line 4.

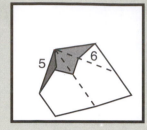

4. Fold corners in along lines 5 and 6, using the middle fold as a guide. Then unfold.

5. Fold the corners in along lines 7 and 8 so that the edges line up along the creases you made in step 4.

6. Fold the corners in again along lines 9 and 10, then refold along lines 5 and 6.

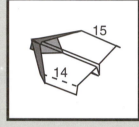

7. Fold the tip over along line 11, then refold the plane down the middle.

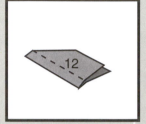

8. Fold the wings down along lines 12 and 13.

9. Fold the wingtips down along lines 14 and 15.

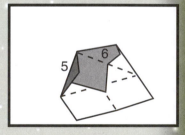

**Finished Airplane**

# Firefly

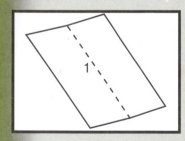

1. Fold paper in half length-wise along line 1, then unfold it.

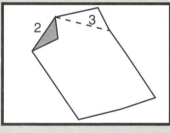

2. Fold the corners in along lines 2 and 3.

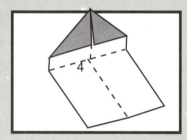

3. Fold the tip up along line 4.

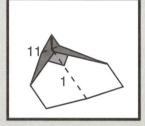

4. Fold the corners in along lines 5 and 6.

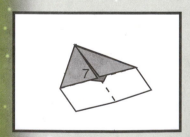

5. Fold the triangle-shaped tip up along line 7.

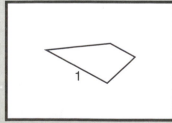

6. Fold the plane in half along the center line folded in step 1.

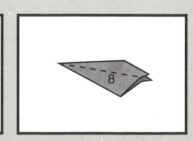

7. Fold the wings down along lines 8 and 9.

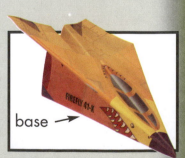

**Finished Airplane**

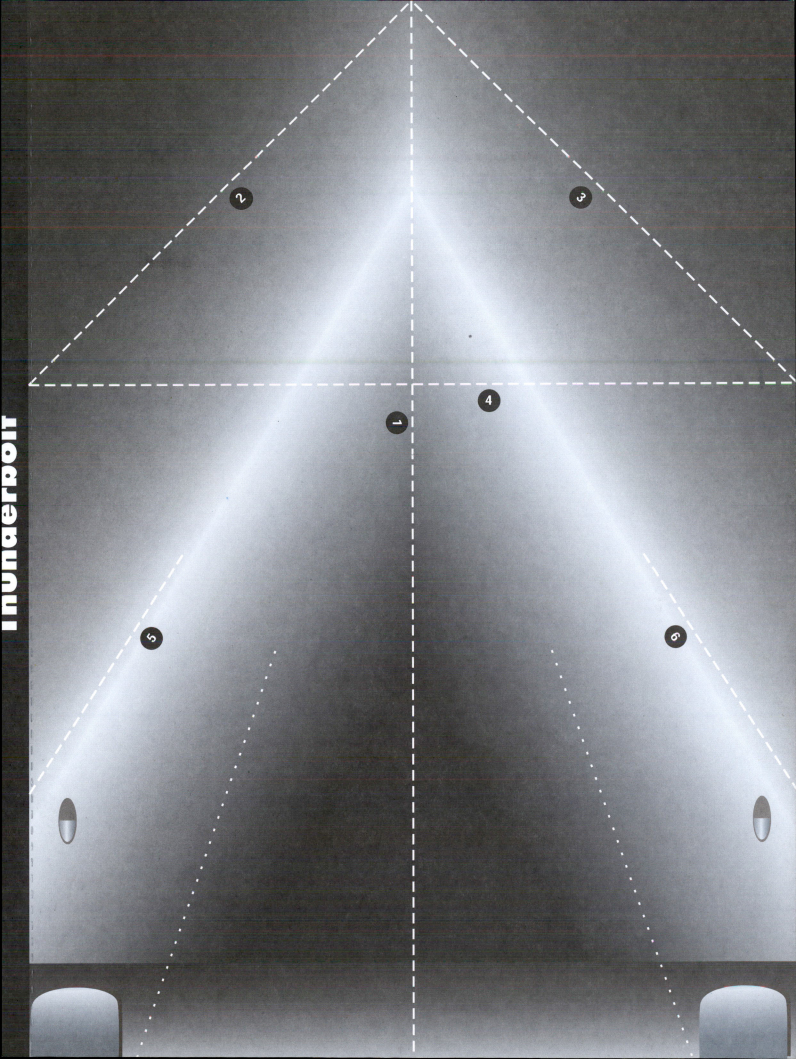

THUNDERBOLT XG1

THUNDERBOLT XG1

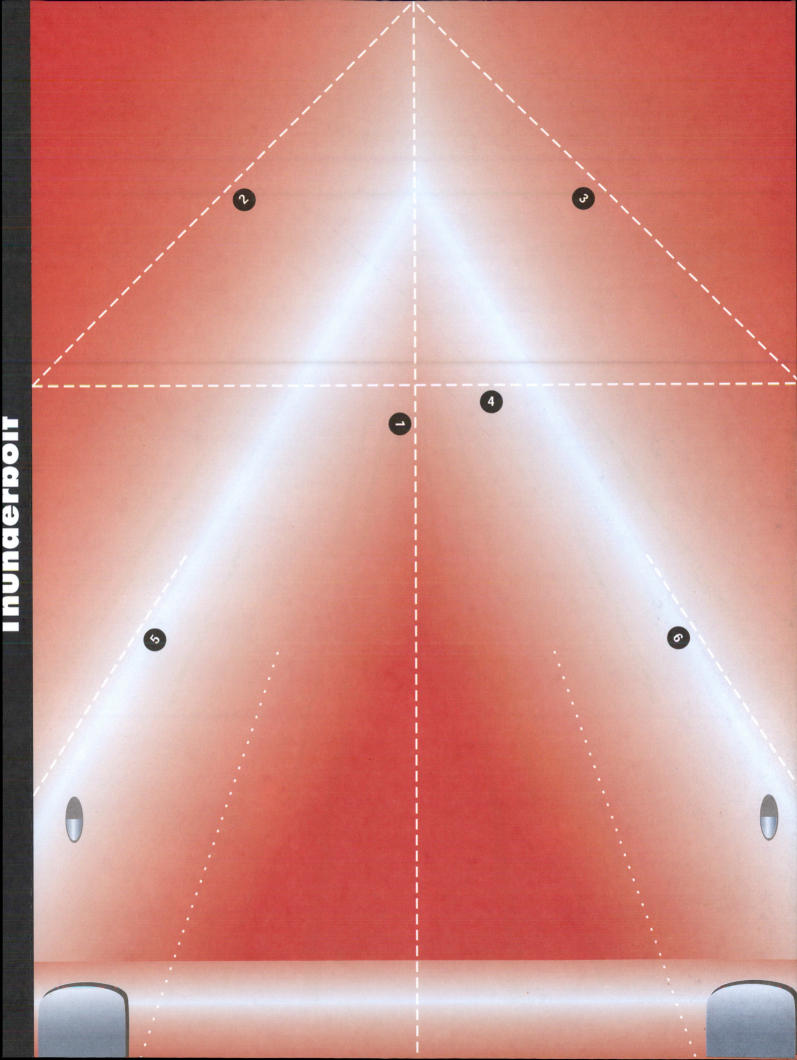

THUNDERBOLT XG1

THUNDERBOLT XG1

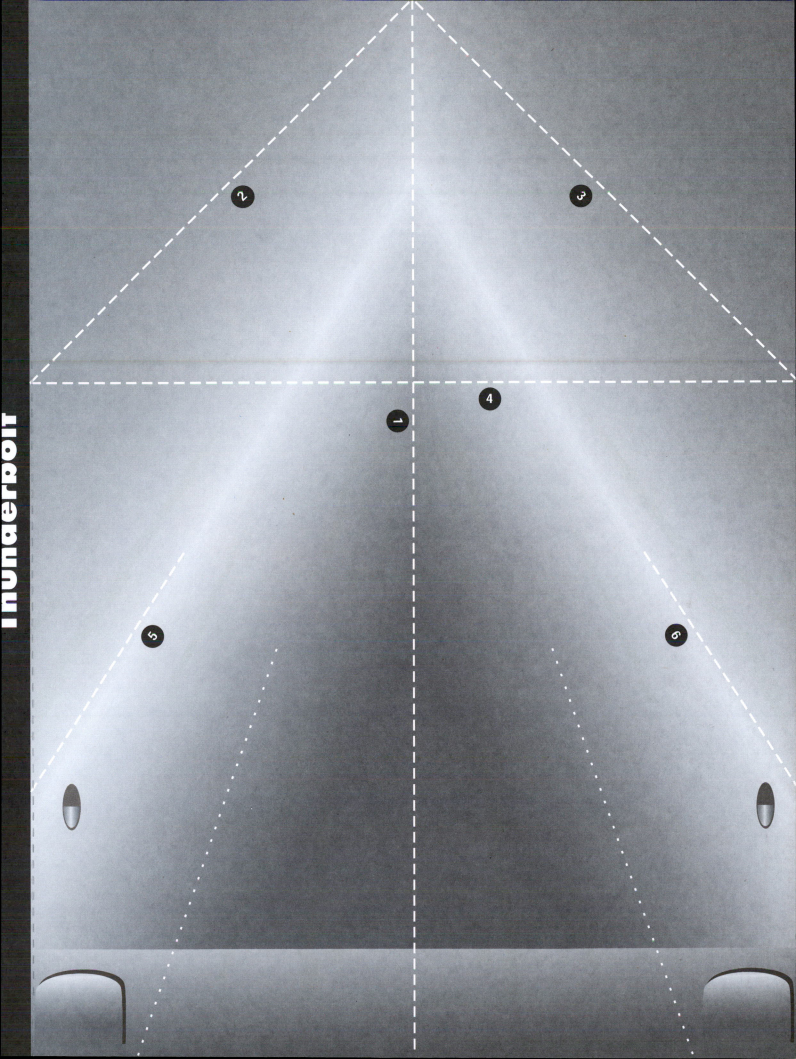

THUNDERBOLT XG1

THUNDERBOLT XG1

Thunderbolt

Aurora

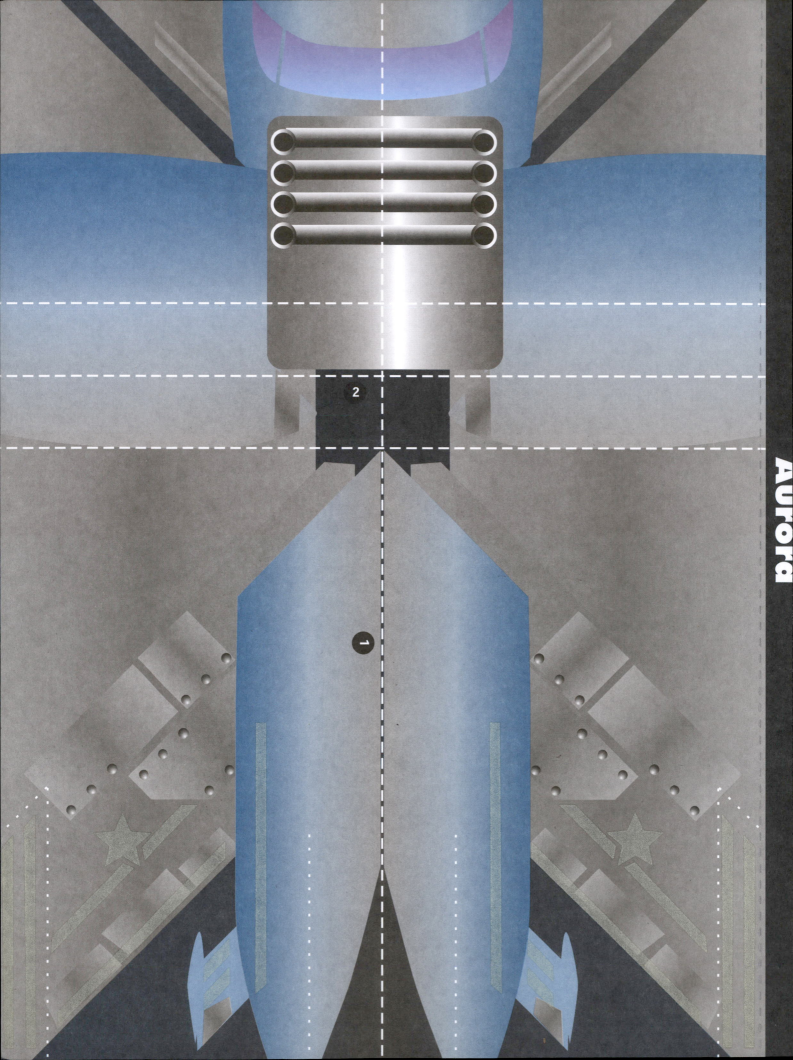

Aurora

Aurora

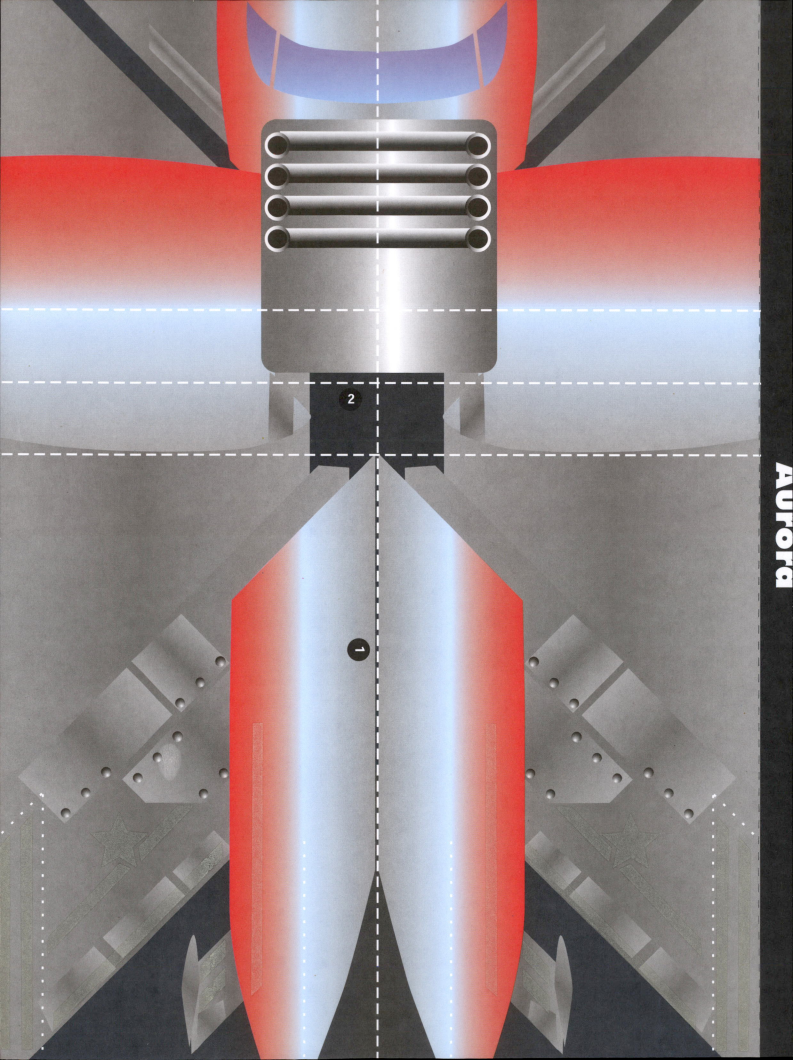

Aurora

# Shooting Star

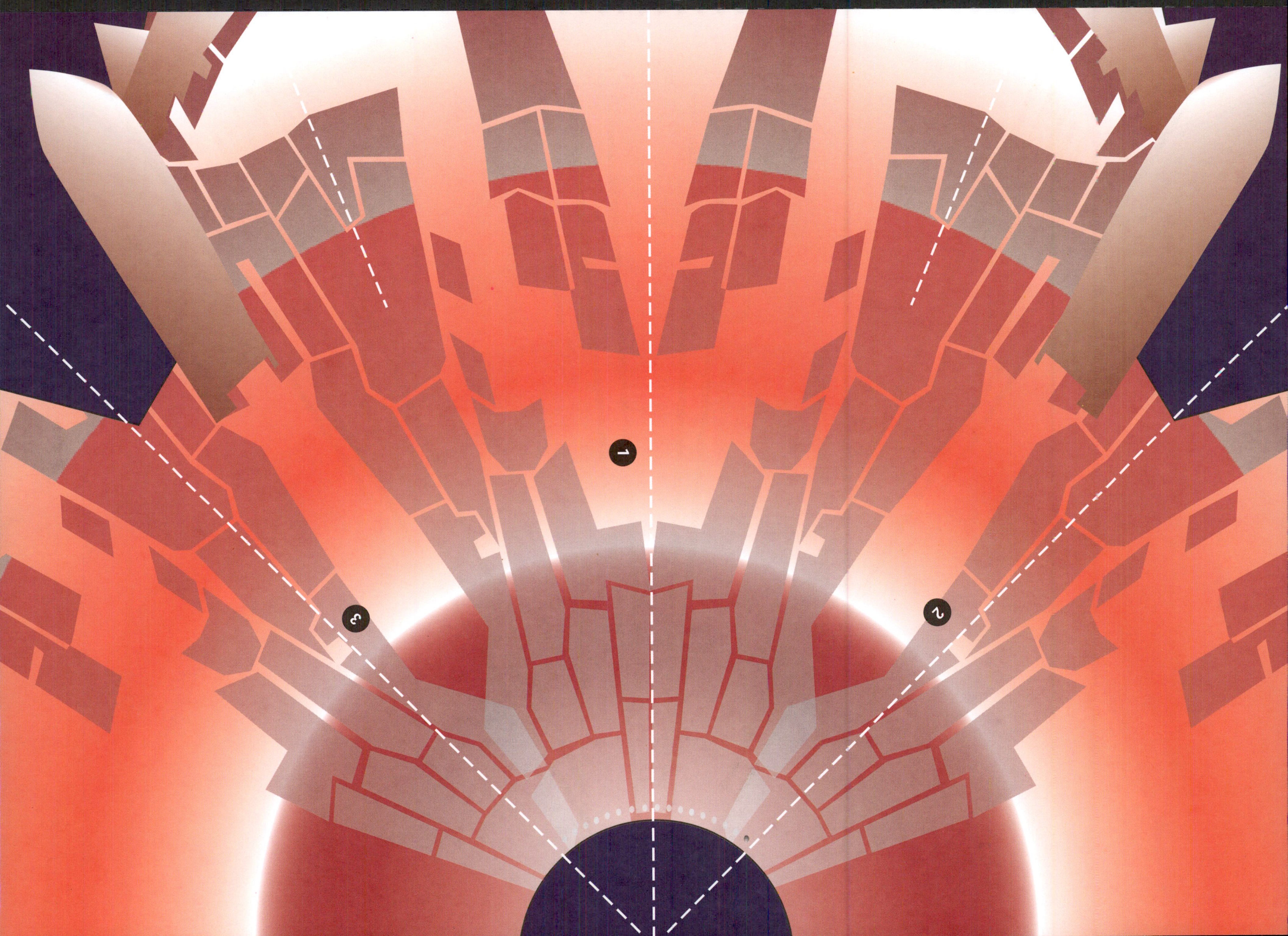

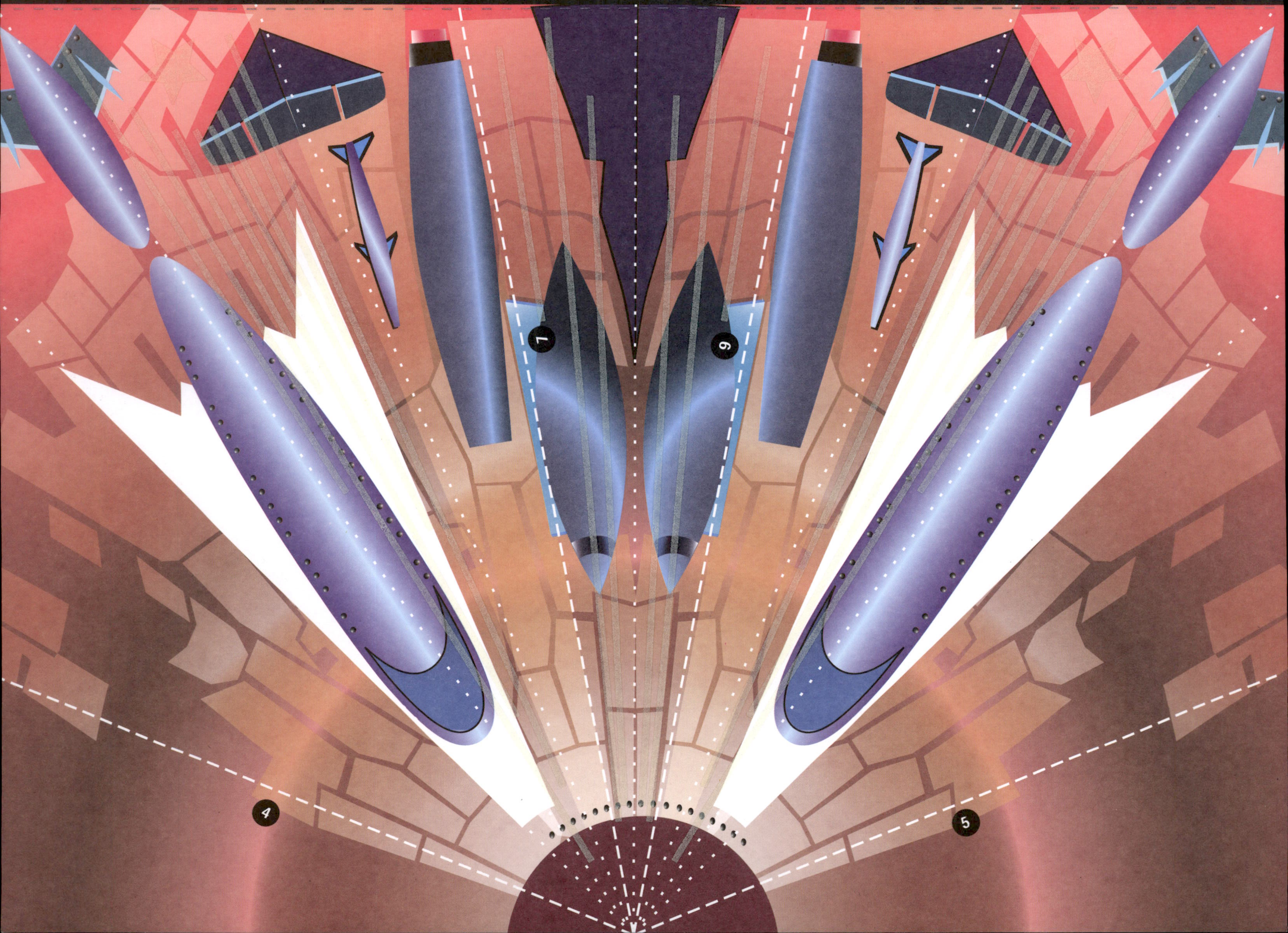
7
6
4
5

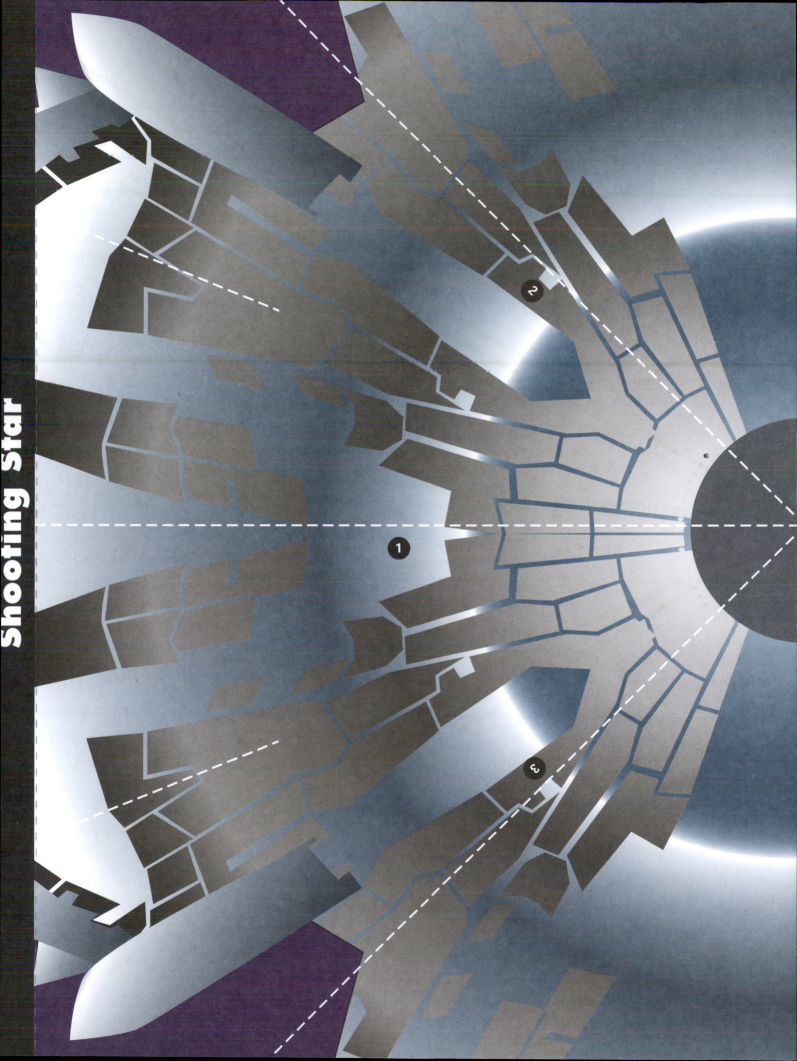

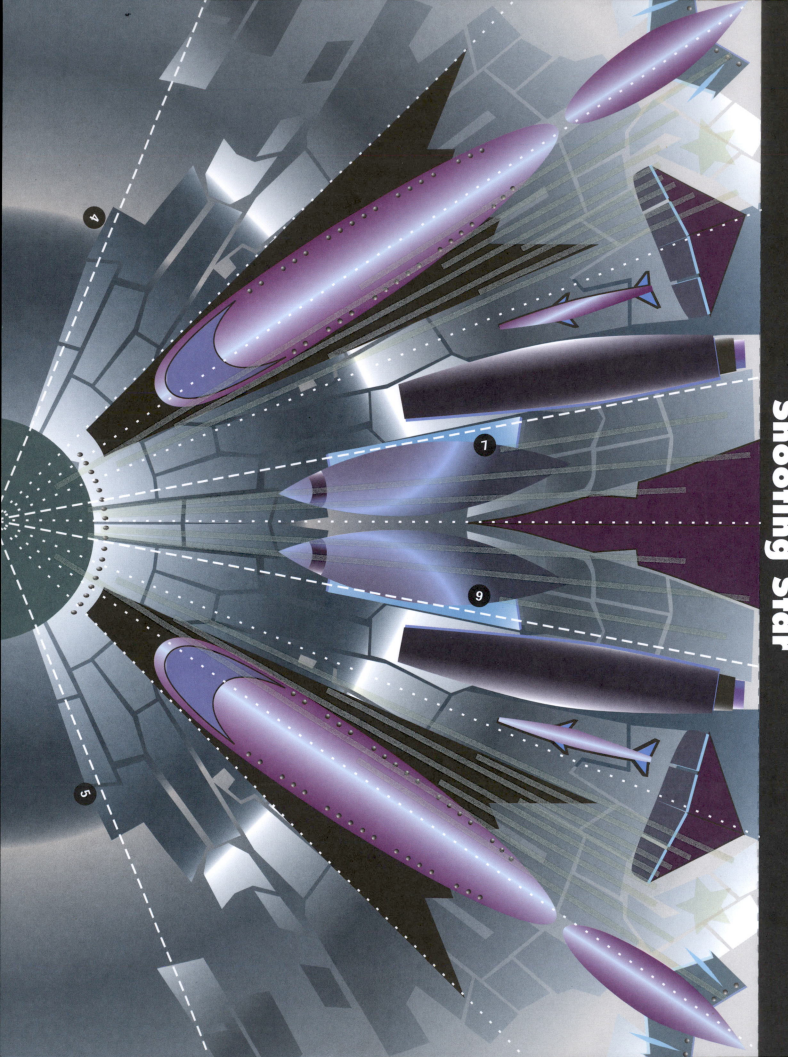

# Shooting Star

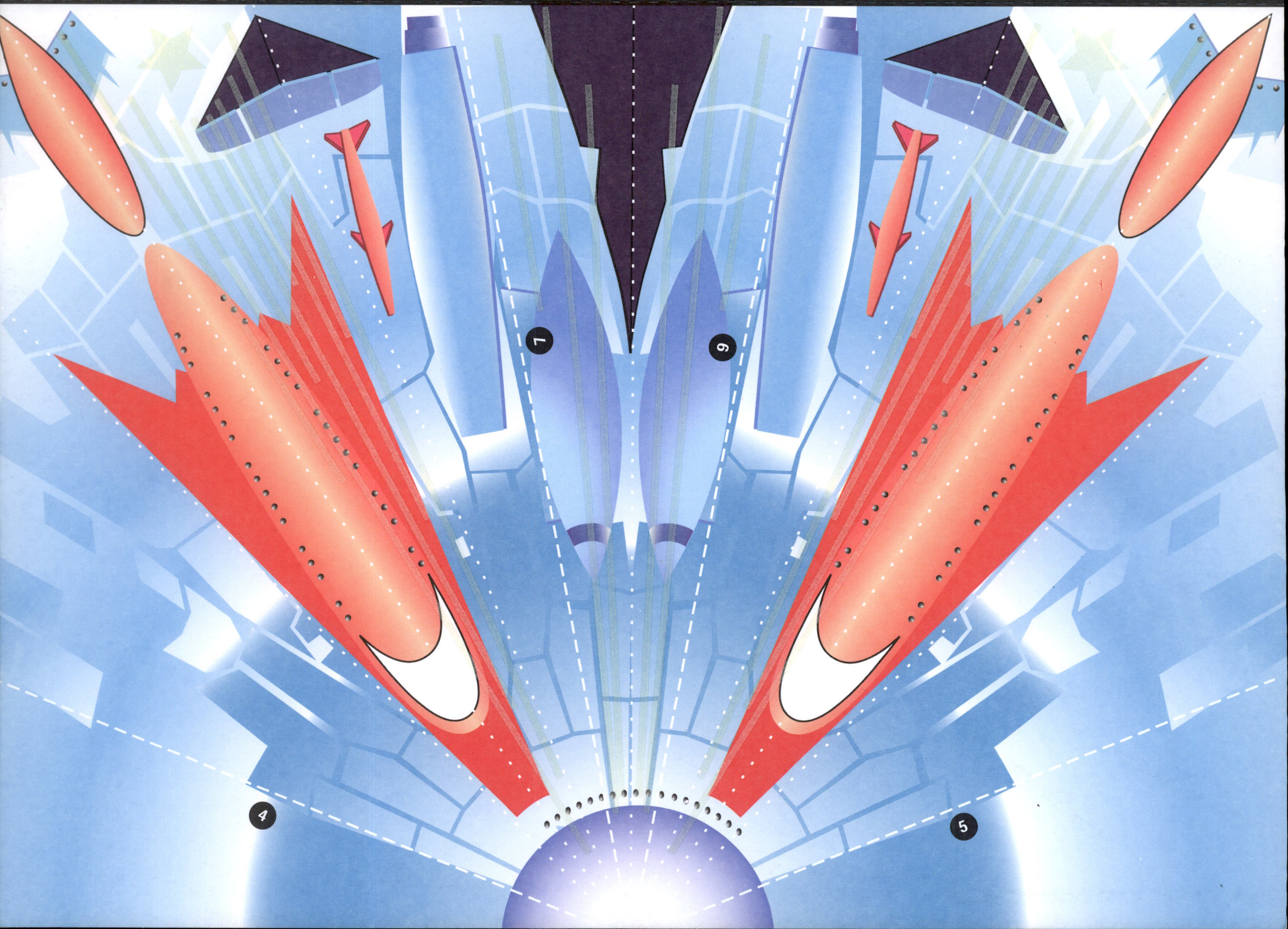

Electric Bat

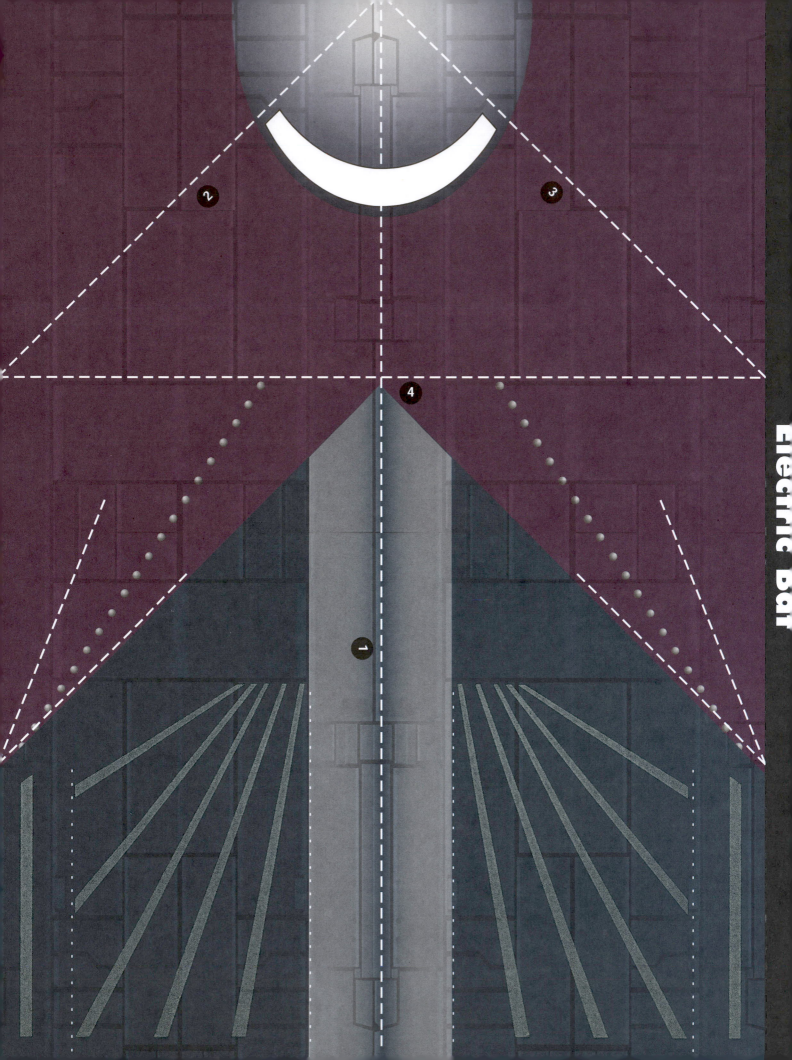

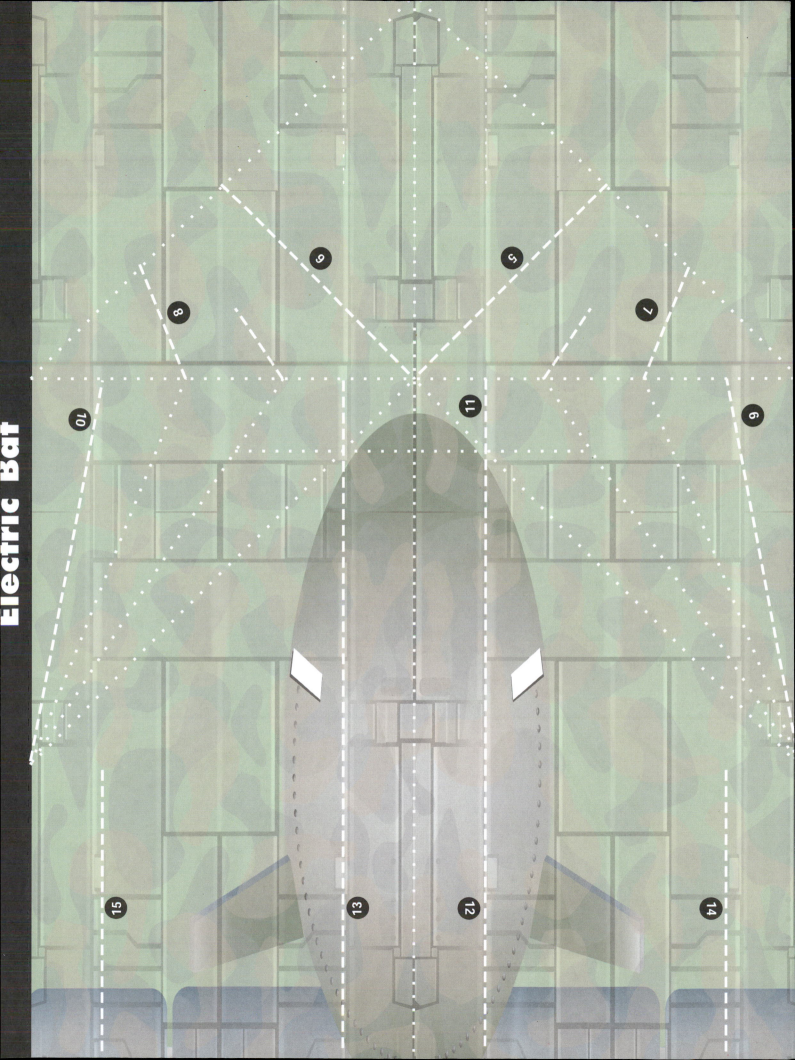

Electric Bat

Electric Bat

Electric Bat

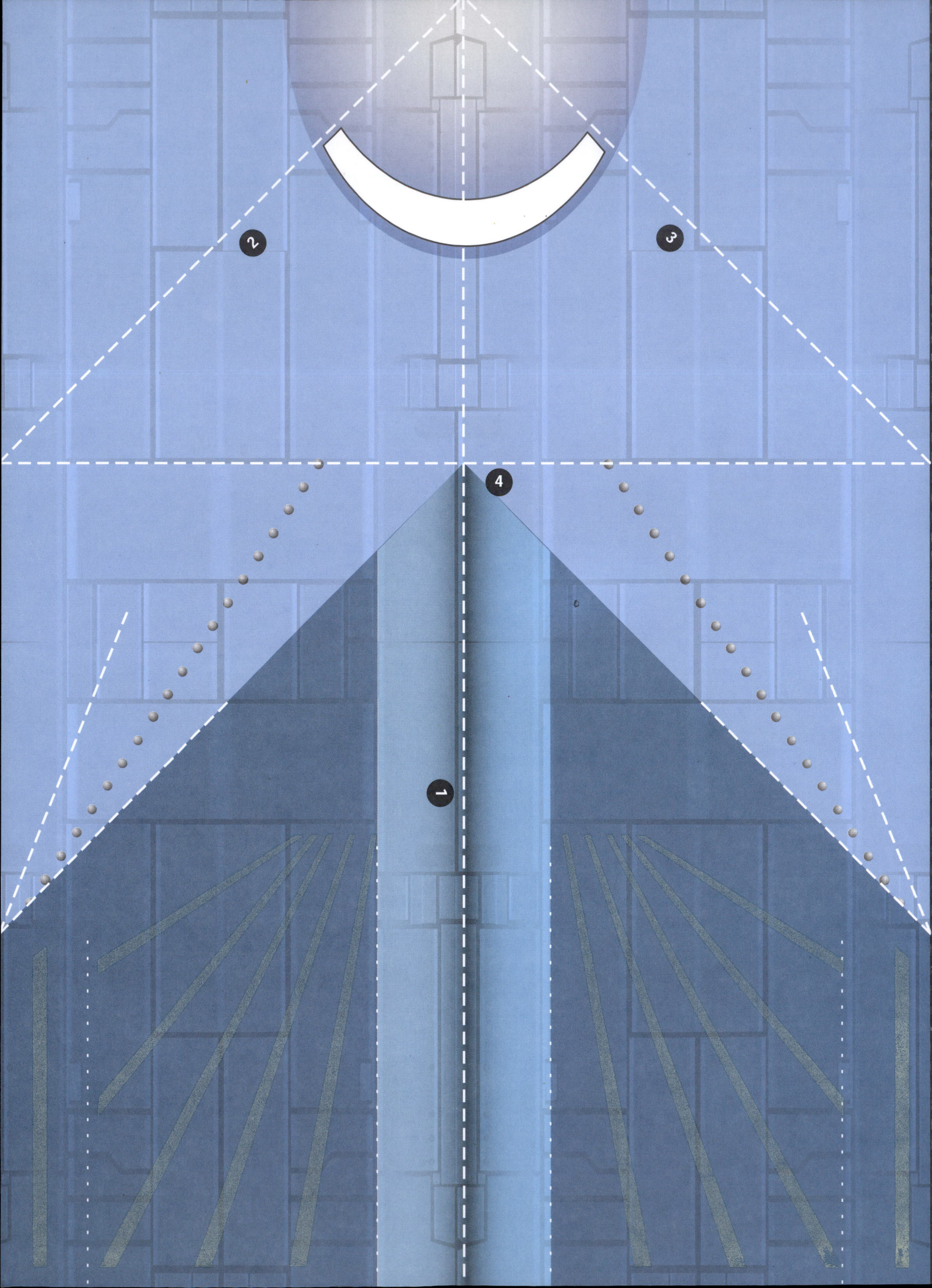


Electric Bat

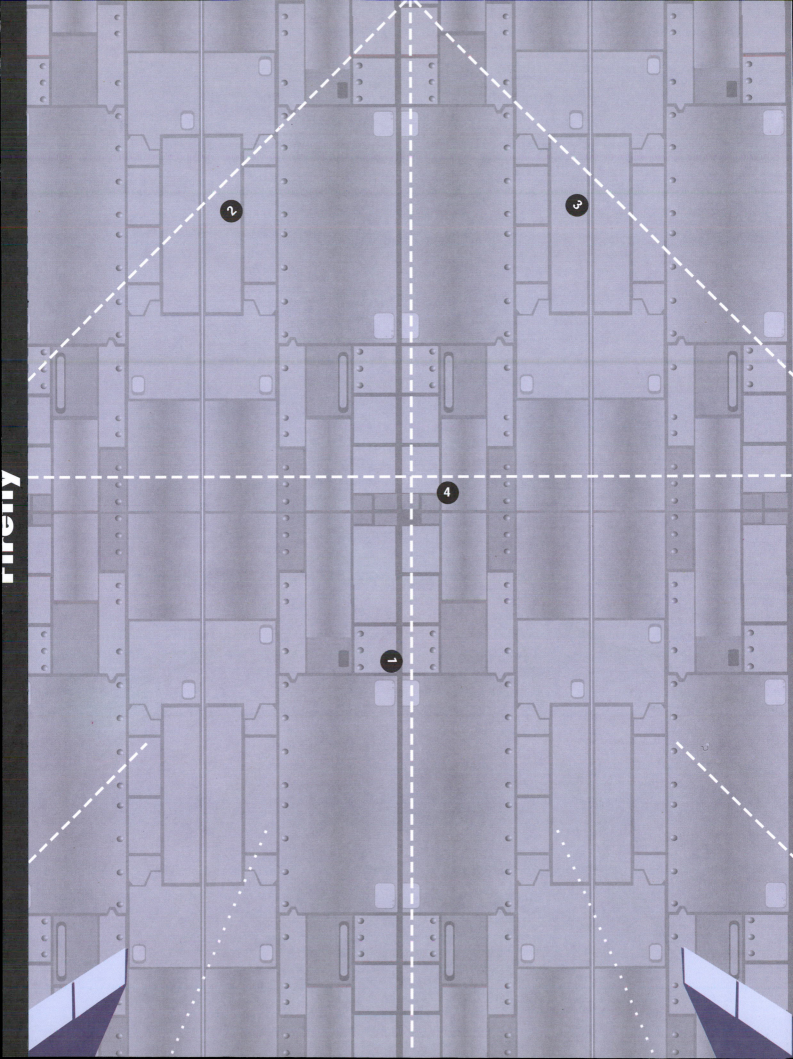

FIREFLY 41-X

FIREFLY 41-X

CAUTION

CAUTION

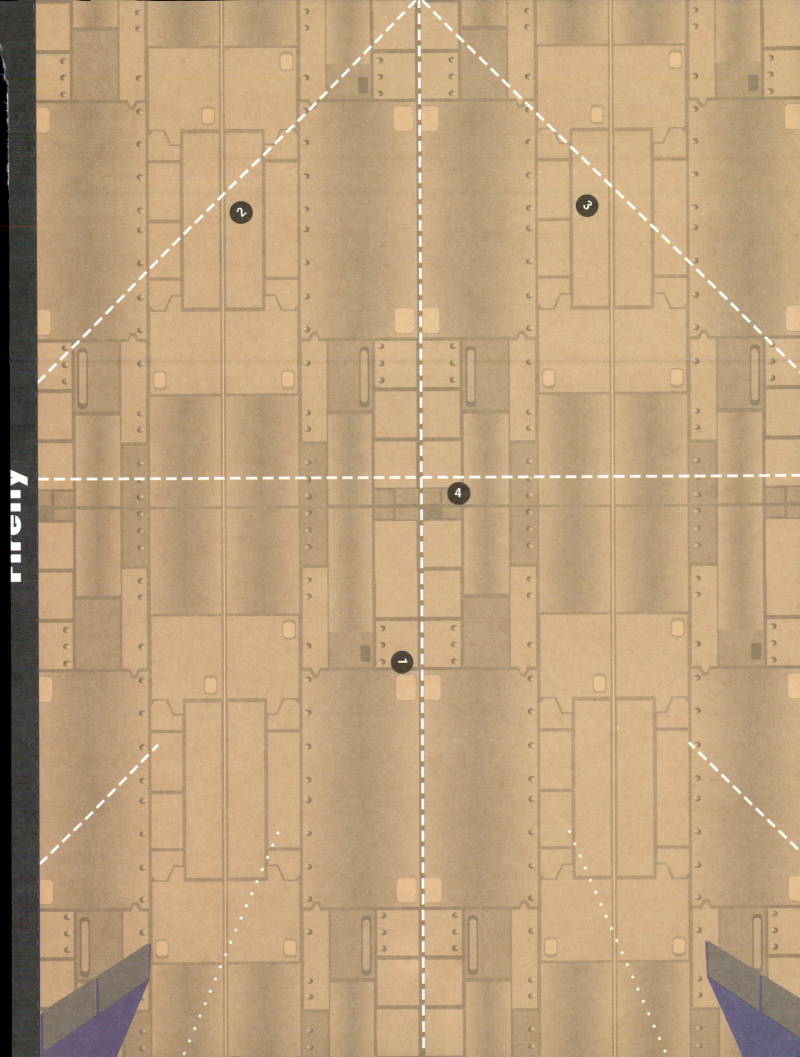

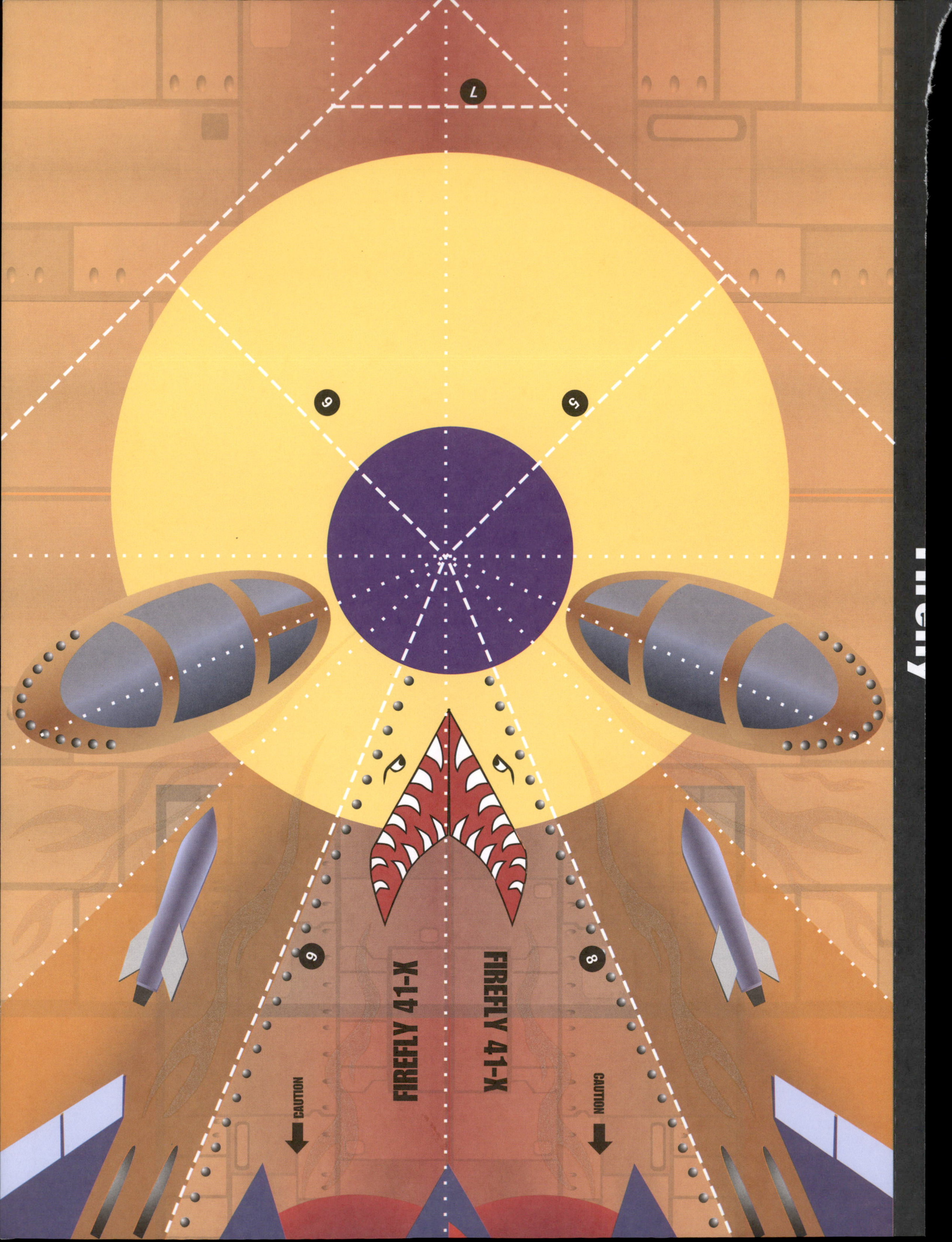
7
6
5
9
8
FIREFLY 41-X
FIREFLY 41-X
CAUTION
CAUTION

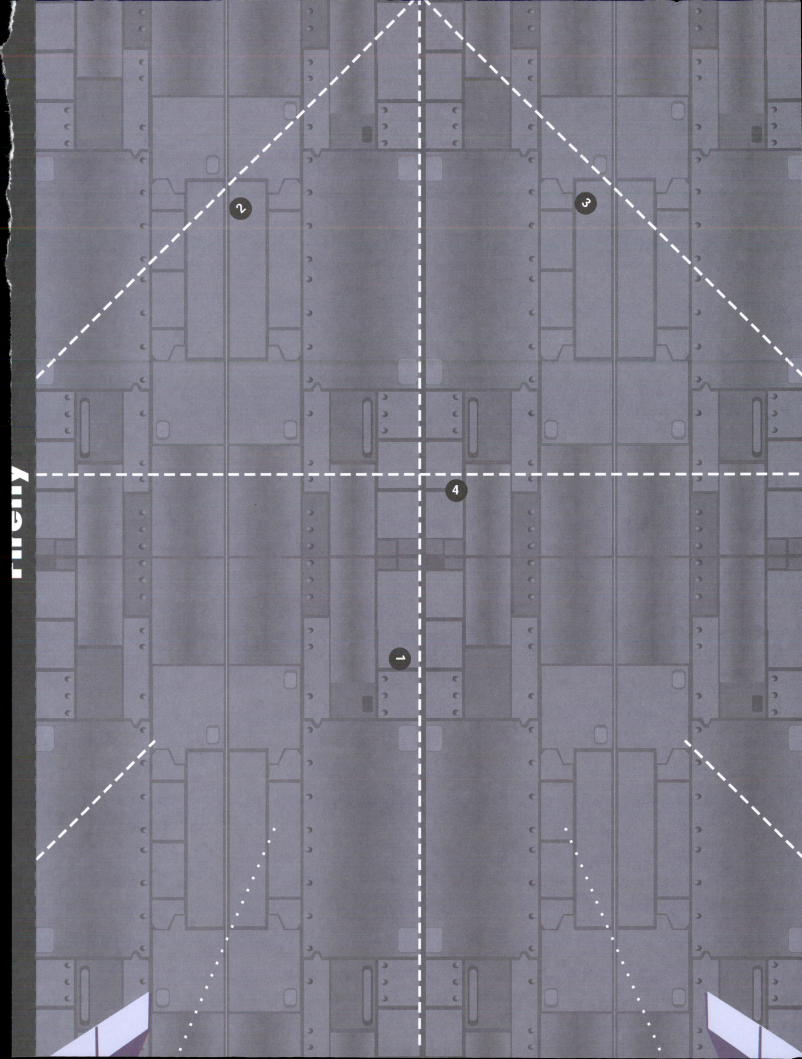

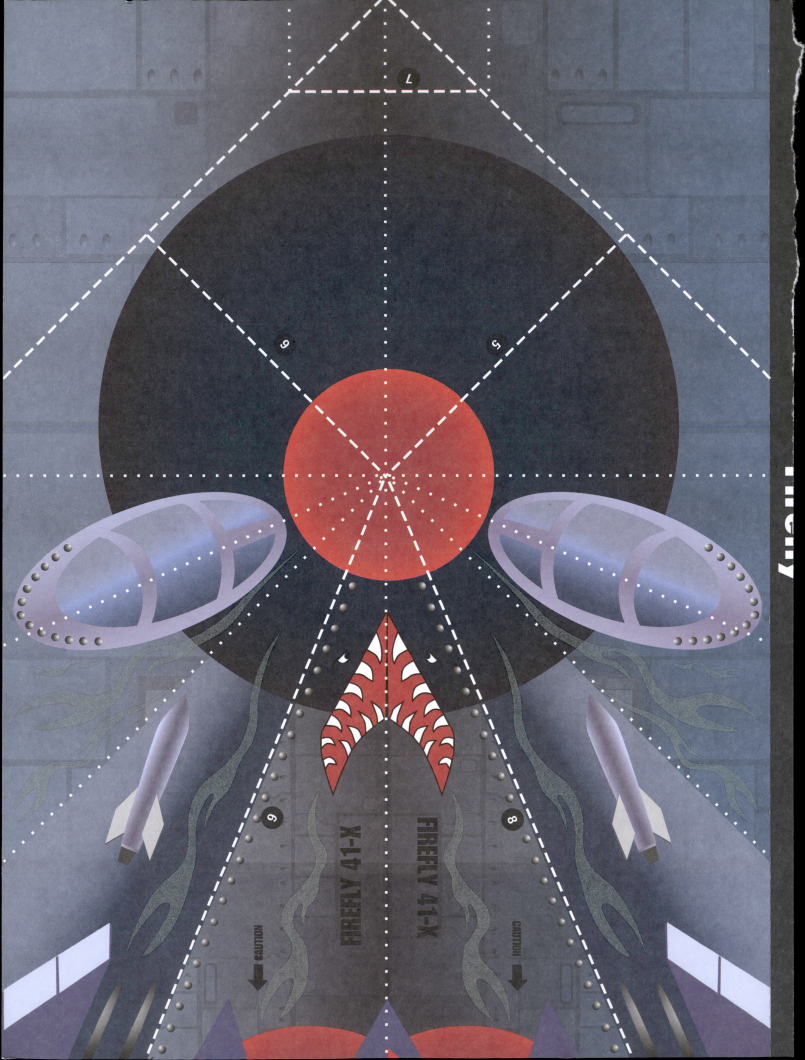